D1524229

THE BOOK OF DEMONOLOGY

Andrew J. Bould

Copyright © 2024 by Andrew J. Bould.

All rights reserved. No part of this book may be reproduced, stored in a retrieval system, or transmitted in any form or by any means, electronic, mechanical, photocopying, recording, or otherwise, without prior written permission from the publisher, except for brief quotations embodied in critical reviews and certain other noncommercial uses permitted by copyright law.

TABLE OF CONTENTS

ECHOES OF DARKNESS: ORIGINS AND LEGENDS OF DEMONOLOGY 6

SACRED OFFERINGS AND MYSTIC OMENS 15

THE SHADOWY REALMS 21

DARK REVELATIONS.. 34

THE PHANTOM PROPHECY 49

THE SPECTRAL LEGACY 58

THE HAUNTING PROPHECY 74

THE PHANTOM RIDER... 86

THE HAUNTING OF PEST.. 91

ECHOES OF DARKNESS: ORIGINS AND LEGENDS OF DEMONOLOGY

To the Chaldeans we owe the primordial whispers of demonology, a dark and ancient art that seeped from the shadows of Chaldea into the veins of Persia, Egypt, and Greece. In the dawn of human consciousness, before the dawn of written history, the belief in spirits and witchcraft thrived, casting its long, eerie shadow across the minds of men. Among these early tales, none is more chilling than the Rabbinical legend of Lilith, the first wife of Adam, a sorceress born of darkness and defiance, the mother of demons.

Lilith, fierce and unyielding, scorned Adam's authority and flouted the divine edicts delivered by celestial messengers. Her rebellion peaked in an act of unspeakable blasphemy; invoking the sacred name of Jehovah through forbidden cabalistic rites, she ascended into the abyss of the night sky and vanished. Her name became a nocturnal curse whispered in fear, for Lilith was believed to steal the breath of infants, a spectral menace in the form of an aërial wraith. Newlywed couples would etch the names of angels upon their walls and inscribe "Begone, Lilith" to guard their homes from her malevolent touch. The legends of Lilith, laden with dread, spread like a pestilence from one culture to another, embedding themselves deeply in the Jewish consciousness, who inscribed their bedposts with "Et zelo Chuizlilith" to ward off her nocturnal terrors.

In the ancient world, the Greeks and Romans spoke of demons not with fear, but with a reverence for the power they wielded—spirits visible to mortals, capable of both benevolence and malevolence. To the Jews and early Christians, however, demons were creatures of pure malevolence, born of unholy unions between humans and the supernatural, or the restless spirits of the dead, returning to haunt the living with vengeance. They classified these spirits into celestial, aquatic, airy, and fiery beings, each with their own sinister purposes. Tertullian warned of spirits that soared faster than any bird, waiting passively until summoned to act, while evil spirits roamed freely at the devil's behest, ready to be commanded by those who knew the dark arts.

The ancient Egyptians harbored a grim legend of their own—an epoch when humanity rebelled against the gods, driving them to seek refuge in Egypt, where they transformed into various beasts. This metamorphosis laid the foundation for the veneration of these creatures. The Arabians, steeped in their own mysticism, believed in genii—spirits that shadowed individuals through life, one good and one evil, locked in eternal combat, reflecting the turmoil within the human soul. Their chief genius, Hafedhah, was invoked for strength and cunning before embarking on raids, a dark prayer for a dark purpose.

In medieval Europe, the dark arts of conjuration flourished, and devils manifested in terrifying forms, blending the sublime with the monstrous. An anonymous chronicler describes these encounters with vivid horror: devils would appear as angels in fiery chariots or ride infernal dragons, clutching vipers, with lion heads, goose feet, and hare tails. Others took the guise of aged warriors astride crocodiles, wielding hooks, or human figures with griffin wings, adorned with three heads—one a toad, another a cat, and the third a fearsome predator with enormous fangs.

These demonic apparitions could be crowned kings upon pale horses with serpentine tails, bearing lances and banners, or warriors on black steeds, shrouded in flames. They could assume the faces of lions with fiery eyes or ride forth in regal splendor on crimson steeds. Each form more terrifying and grotesque than the last, a parade of nightmarish visions designed to strike fear into the hearts of mortals.

Thus, through the ages, the dark and epic saga of demons and spirits unfolded, a testament to humanity's ceaseless fascination with the supernatural, and the creeping terror that lies just beyond the veil of reality.

In the shadowy realms beyond mortal comprehension, where light is but a whisper and darkness reigns supreme, the fate of souls is a spectacle of harrowing grandeur. Inferior demons, twisted and malevolent, are tasked with dragging the condemned into the abyss, while ethereal, benevolent spirits escort the blessed from our earthly realm to paradisiacal sanctuaries.

Toledo, Seville, and Salamanca stood as citadels of arcane wisdom. Within their hallowed halls, sorcerers proclaimed that all knowledge could be wrested from the grasp of fallen angels. These arcane masters, versed in abstruse sciences, alchemy, the myriad tongues of men and beasts, divinity, magic, and prophecy, wielded the power to command the elements, influence celestial bodies, and incite cataclysms. They claimed dominion over earthquakes, pestilence, and even the delicate balance of life and death, professing the ability to liberate souls from purgatory, sway human passions, reconcile or divide allies, and induce madness or melancholy.

In the twilight of life, the Circassians shielded their dead from evil spirits by anointing graves with holy water and tolling bells. They believed fervently that the departed remained aware of worldly affairs, prompting affectionate kin to revisit burial grounds, reciting prayers for the deceased's repose.

As an Indian teetered on the brink of death, a Brahmin's prayers filled the air, invoking the presence of dueling spirits—one benevolent, the other malevolent. The virtuous were whisked away in chariots of light to realms of eternal joy, while the wicked were seized by the dark spirits and dragged before a tribunal of fearsome judgment. Condemned souls roamed the earth as magpies for ten days, compelling the living to feed these birds, believing them to be the incarnations of their departed loved ones.

Deep beneath the earth lay hell, where Yhamadar presided, with Xitragupten chronicling every mortal deed. This infernal president dispensed justice with brutal fairness, sending some souls back to inhabit lesser forms, while others faced unimaginable torments in the underworld. In their final moments, the dying clung to a cow's tail while a Brahmin performed sacred rites, offering money to safeguard the soul from demonic grasp.

In Pegu, copper vessels and bells echoed through the night to repel restless demons disturbing the dead. Priests, claiming an understanding of demonic desires, sought to placate these dark entities with grand feasts, where the friends of the ailing danced to haunting melodies. They believed that devils, with bodies and souls akin to humans, could foretell futures and instigate dreams, consulting them much like the witches of Britain did.

On death's threshold in Cochin-China, warriors

brandished their sabres around the dying, believing demons lurked to snatch away the soul. When a prince perished, a grim conclave of priests would identify the demon responsible and condemn it to eternal damnation. In the Molucca Islands, people believed in dual angels guiding each life—one towards virtue, the other towards ruin. These guardians influenced every action, with the air worshipped under the name Lanitho, subject to the spirit Lanthila. Under the veil of night, they would summon their gods, invoking mysterious incantations to foresee the future, a power passed down through select families.

Ravaged by smallpox, the people erected grotesque effigies atop their homes to ward off the disease-spreading demon. Encountering a funeral or a corpse filled them with dread, especially for women carrying children, fearing the hovering soul of the deceased sought to harm the living. To shield their offspring from malevolent forces, they adorned their infants with charmed beads and slept with consecrated artifacts under their pillows, living in perpetual fear of the demonic, and constantly striving to thwart their sinister schemes.

SACRED OFFERINGS AND MYSTIC OMENS

In the shadowed heart of ancient Ceylon, when the prayers of the heathens fell upon deaf ears, they would venture into the most foreboding corners of their sacred groves. There, among the twisted trees and whispering winds, they offered blood-red cocks to the devil, where they believed he and his malevolent minions reveled. In times of sickness, a red cock was consecrated to one of their genii, with the priest solemnly declaring that the sacrifice was contingent upon the recovery of the afflicted. The offerings, it was believed, ascended to the heavens to be presented to Buddha himself. To unmask the spirit—be it benevolent or malevolent—that plagued the sick, a bow crafted from the first found stick was prepared. A small chisel dangled from the bowstring, and as the priest named every god and devil he could conjure, the bow would spin at the mention of the spirit responsible. These mystic bows were also said to foretell future events, the air heavy with foreboding and dread.

Among the schismatic Greeks, infants, unbaptized, were thought to harbor unclean spirits. Before baptism, the priest would cross the child, commanding the devil to flee. A cross of gold, silver, or tin was then hung around the child's neck, a talisman to be worn until death. Woe to the one found without this sacred emblem upon death; such bodies were cast into the earth without the sanctity of sacred rites.

The negroes revered fetishes akin to the Manitous of the North Americans and the ancient Fauns of the Romans. Birds, fishes, and trees were considered fetishes, guardians of hills, mountains, and streams. The breaking of a sacred tree's branch was believed to doom their crops to destruction. Fetishes were their oracles, appearing as black dogs to deliver their cryptic messages. Large fetishes protected homes, while smaller ones, worn around the neck or concealed under armpits, offered personal protection. Charms and sacred rings adorned the bodies of their children to ward off evil spirits. Thursdays were devoted to fetish worship, where priests, versed in the dark arts, instructed the people. At death, it was believed they transformed into serpents, thus these reptiles were never harmed.

The Gaures, shunning the earth's pollution by decomposing bodies, placed their dead in round towers, accessed only through apertures in the roof. For three days, friends vigilantly watched over the body to prevent its seizure by the devil. By the fourth day, the soul's fate was sealed—either in torment or bliss. This determination was made by observing vultures feast upon the body; the right eye's consumption signified bliss, while the left portended torment. Alternatively, the proximity of a dog to the corpse revealed the soul's fate.

In Madagascar, diverse orders of genii governed the stars, planets, and elements. Spirits, both male and female, intermarried and produced offspring, revealing future events and performing superhuman feats. The natives believed in phantoms and ghosts, warding off evil with ritualistic dances and javelins.

The Floridans, too, worshipped the devil in myriad forms. In the Caribbee Islands, bats were seen as supernatural guardians of the night. Relics of the dead were consulted for guidance, while the Boias, or native priests, summoned their genii by burning tobacco and chanting incantations in the darkness. These genii were called upon to diagnose and predict the outcomes of illnesses, their presence signaled by the appearance of black dogs.

The Brazilians' domestic gods were consulted through their priests, who were also fortune-tellers and dream interpreters. They left provisions at graves to sustain the spirits of the deceased, believing this nourishment would prevent their spirits from dying.

The Peruvians spoke of Choun, a being of extraordinary power who reshaped the landscape and commanded the elements. Offended by the people, he transformed fertile lands into deserts but later, in a rare moment of mercy, restored the springs and rivers. Worship shifted to the mightier Pachacamac, who transformed Choun's followers into wild beasts. The people drew omens from the heavens, interpreting comets and rainbows, dreams and earthly signs.

In the Americas, devil worship prevailed, demons manifesting in various forms. In France, Satan's minions—witches, imps, and malevolent spirits— spread fear and chaos. At Lyons, he appeared as a beguiling woman, leading many into sin. In 1612, in Paris, a devil disguised as a beautiful woman enticed men into scandalous acts, only to be revealed as the spirit of a recently hanged woman. At St. Steven's Church in Mascon, graves were disturbed, the dead raised, and the vintage destroyed by the devil's hand.

The Greeks and Romans believed that upon death, each man possessed three spirits: the Manes, descending to the underworld; the Anima, ascending to the skies; and the Umbra, lingering by the tomb, unwilling to part from the body, a spectral shadow in eternal unrest.

THE SHADOWY REALMS

In the twilight of human history, when shadows danced on the walls of civilization, belief in the spectral and unseen was as pervasive as the air itself. Before and after the tumultuous epochs of the Middle Ages, the world was a canvas for apparitions and witchcraft. A venerable cleric of our own land proclaimed with conviction, "It is a deliberate act of divine will that sporadic, vivid manifestations of ghosts and witchcraft serve to jolt and awaken the torpid, dreamlike minds of the populace, compelling them to acknowledge, if not fully believe, in the existence of entities beyond our mortal coil. In this, the divine providence surely intertwines with the malevolent forces of the dark realm, allowing nefarious men and women, and wayward spirits of that shadowy dominion, to forge sinister pacts and confess their wicked deeds, thus providing tangible proof that evil spirits are as real as the good ones."

In the previous century, Theophilus Insulanus, an author of arcane lore, decreed that doubting the reality of ghostly apparitions was a mark of irreligion. His conviction held that those who questioned the spectral manifestations of departed souls were bereft of faith. Another scholar of the supernatural posited that ghosts were ethereal beings, devoid of substance, capable of passing through walls and solid matter at will. These phantoms often appeared in the garb of their living selves, though occasionally shrouded in white, their presence heralded by an inexplicable glow. Dogs and horses, gifted with a unique perception, were often witnesses to these ghostly visitations.

On the shores of the Baltic, a deity named Putseet held sway, invoked by nightly offerings of bread, butter, cheese, and ale left in barns. Should these provisions vanish by dawn, good fortune was foretold; if untouched, misfortune loomed. This spirit labored in the dead of night, aiding in tasks such as thrashing, churning, grinding, and sweeping.

Among the Northern tribes, spirits of this ilk were seen as the souls of those who had indulged in forbidden pleasures during their lifetimes, condemned to roam the earth, assisting the living as penance.

A chilling legend from Germany tells of brass gates with a fissure, a result of a devilish encounter. When an emperor decreed the construction of a church, Satan himself inquired of its purpose. Deceptively, the emperor declared it a gaming house, to which the devil agreed to lend his aid. Upon discovering altars within, Satan, tricked and enraged, flung a pair of brass gates so violently that one was damaged. These gates became relics, drawing the curious for generations.

In Western Europe, superstition bred numerous formidable demons, their origins woven from

Celtic, Teutonic, and Eastern myths. In Orkney, even a century ago, lovers pledged themselves within sacred stone circles dedicated to Scandinavian gods. They clasped hands through a stone's hole, vowing their love in the name of Odin. Breaking this vow branded one as infamous for eternity.

From the colossal body of the giant Ymir, maggots transformed by divine command into beings of both human form and intellect. These diminutive creatures, mentioned in earlier pages, with their exquisite figures, resided in subterranean lairs or rocky clefts. Known for their wealth, agility, and malice, they were likely the ancestors of modern fairies, described as diminutive and flamboyantly attired. These offspring of worms wielded the power to become visible or invisible at will. They lived in unparalleled splendor, befriending some humans while tormenting others. With their elf arrows, they could strike down man and beast alike, abducting children and animals, often replacing them with grotesque replicas to mask their crimes.

In the ancient and shadowed lands of this once-naive realm, the legends of the dwarfs have shifted, taking on a darker, more enigmatic hue. Once akin to the ethereal Persian peris, these diminutive beings were believed to bestow bounties upon England. They whispered dreams into the ears of the sleeping, conjured wealth from the void, and wove prosperity into the very fabric of the nation. In those primordial days, every grand household in Ireland and the Highland realms of Scotland harbored a brownie—a spectral guardian, as varied in stature as humankind. These brownies, steadfast and tireless, demanded respectful homage, much like the ancient Samogitæ revered their Putseet. Once a brownie pledged itself to a family, it bound its spectral essence to their lineage, haunting and aiding generation after generation.

Burton, the sage of the eldritch, speaks of nine infernal classes: the false deities of pagans, revered in dark idols, who murmured oracles at

Delphos and beyond, ruled by the dread Beelzebub; the deceivers and double-talkers like Apollo and Pythias; the architects of chaos, such as Plato's Theutus; malevolent fiends of vengeance, commanded by Asmodeus; the tricksters of magic and sorcery, under Satan's command; the aërial phantoms that poisoned the air, sowing plagues, thunder, fire, and catastrophe; the harbingers of destruction, igniting wars and unrest; the sinister accusers driving souls to despair; and the tempters, shape-shifters with Mammon as their prince. Burton delves deeper, proclaiming that the world teems with spirits, devils, and entities unseen. No inch is void, not in the heavens, earth, nor the waters above and below. The earth swarms with devils far more than with summer's flies.

Psellus, the master of demonology, devised a chilling taxonomy of demons, grounded in their nature and abodes. His first category comprised fiery demons, drifting near the moon's pale glow, yet barred from its sanctuary. These entities flared in blazing stars, mimic suns, moons, and spectral lights, warding off foul weather. They sometimes sought refuge in the infernos of Hecla, Etna, or Vesuvius. His second category encompassed aërial demons, dwelling in the sky, conjuring storms, thunder, and lightning. These fiends splintered trees, incinerated steeples and homes, smote men and beasts, and rained stones, wool, and frogs from the heavens. They staged spectral battles in the clouds, summoned whirlwinds and fire, and tainted the air to unleash plagues.

The third class were the earthbound devils—lares, genii, fauns, satyrs, wood-nymphs, foliots, robin-goodfellows, or trulli—spirits tied to the forest and field. The fourth class included aqueous devils, various water nymphs haunting the depths. The fifth class were subterranean demons, known as Getuli or Cobals, hoarding treasures in the earth, guarding them with terrible ferocity, and causing violent earthquakes to deter intruders. Psellus's sixth class, the lucifugi, thrived in darkness, infesting the bodies of the living, driving their hosts to madness and seizures. It was whispered that these devils possessed physical forms, able to feel and inflict harm, nourished by strange sustenance, not from malice, but to draw vital heat and moisture from the creatures they slaughtered. They shunned the sun's rays and aged imperceptibly over countless years.

In this modern epic of shadow and flame, where unseen forces battle for dominion over the mortal realm, the echoes of these ancient beliefs still linger, chilling the very soul and casting long, eerie shadows over the land.

Among the legions of shadowy entities that haunt the chronicles of mankind, none evoke such visceral dread as the vampires. Behold, as Horst describes these abominations: "Cadavers that defy the finality of death, slumbering within their tombs, only to rise under the veil of night. They emerge to feast upon the lifeblood of the living, sustaining their unholy existence and preserving their vile forms from decay, unlike the mortal dead." Fischer, a staunch believer in these nocturnal predators, reveals a chilling truth: a vampire's bite leaves no trace upon its prey, yet swiftly brings death, unless the victim consumes the very soil from the fiend's grave and anoints themselves with its accursed blood. These desperate acts offer but fleeting reprieve; for those bitten are doomed to succumb, their bodies interred only to rise again, perpetuating the cycle of bloodlust and dread.

Even into the heart of the 18th century, vampirism cast its pall over Eastern Europe. This harrowing superstition gnawed at the collective psyche, as none could predict when they might fall prey to these abhorrent fiends and be cursed with the transformation into a vampire. Esteemed men of science lent credence to the existence of vampires, their grave assertions casting a veneer of legitimacy over a subject more suited to the realm of nightmares.

In England, it was whispered that every man possessed a "double" or "fetch," an ethereal doppelgänger whose appearance foretold dire misfortune or imminent death. The mere sighting of this spectral twin would instill profound dread in the observer, a harbinger of doom unshakable in its certainty.

Churchyards across England held their own spectral guardians, phantoms bound to vigil over the unshriven dead—those who met violent ends bereft of sacred rites. In both Scotland and England, the souls of suicides were entangled in a web of dark superstition. Edicts forbade the opening of graveyard gates to these forsaken corpses, compelling kin to surreptitiously transport the bodies over the cemetery walls under the shroud of dusk. More often, the remains of suicides and murderers were consigned to the desolate crossroads, impaled with a stake through their heartless chests, a grim measure to thwart their spirits from rising, to terrify and torment the innocent.

These rites and beliefs are but fragments of a world enshrouded in fear and darkness, where the line between the living and the dead is perilously thin, and the shadow of the supernatural looms ever large, ready to ensnare the unwary in its chilling embrace.

The ritual of driving a stake through the heart of a corpse did not always silence the restless dead, for countless stories speak of phantoms haunting the vicinity of those accursed burial grounds. In a land where the shadows of witchcraft still cling to the people's souls, where not so long ago the laws against witches were enforced with zealous fervor, this is no surprise. The State and the Church both trembled before the dark forces of demons and witches, believing them to walk among us.

The great reformer Luther, whose words still echo through the ages, revealed his dread and knowledge of these evil spirits in his Colloquia. "Many devils," he proclaimed, "lurk in the forests, skulk in the waters, dwell in the wastelands, and hide in the shadowy, swampy places, poised to harm and afflict the unsuspecting. They gather in the thick, black clouds, bringing forth storms of hail, lightning, and thunder, spreading their poison through the air, the fields, and the very earth beneath our feet."

In a chilling discourse on witchcraft, Luther confessed his merciless stance against witches: he would burn every last one of them. He reminded his followers that, under the ancient law, it was the priests who cast the first stones at such damned souls. His own mother had suffered torment at the hands of a neighbor, a witch who could cast a spell upon a child, causing it to wail endlessly until death. A righteous pastor, daring to punish this vile sorceress, met a grim fate when she ensnared him with a curse. Using earth upon which he had walked, she struck him with a malady beyond any remedy's reach, leading to his untimely demise.

Luther was certain that the devil, through his dark prophets, could and did predict the future; that this malevolent being was so cunning he could bring death with merely the leaf of a tree. The devil's arsenal, Luther believed, brimmed with more poisons than all the world's apothecaries had cures. This master of deception could twist our senses, making us see what was not there, hear thunder or trumpets that never sounded. He argued that men were possessed by the devil, both in body and spirit. Those afflicted corporeally were the mad, driven to insanity by the infernal grip of these demonic forces.

DARK REVELATIONS

In the shadowed halls of ancient belief, the Roman Catholic Church weaved a doctrine that spoke of countless malevolent entities, whispering their dark imaginings into the minds of men. These sinister spirits, it was taught, painted vile visions and phantasms in the human imagination, leading the unwary into the abyss. The realm of Satan, a kingdom shrouded in eternal night, ensnared those who dared to submit to the prince of darkness. Magicians, sorcerers, and the forsakers of baptism willingly chained themselves to his dread empire, becoming puppets in his infernal play.

Amidst the dim glow of flickering candles in the

seventeenth century, a chilling manual emerged, known as De Instructione Sacerdotum, a guide for the faithful priests who stood against the encroaching dark. Within its pages, an unsettling truth was revealed:

"Magic," it proclaimed, "is but the manipulation of demonic power. The magician himself wields no true might; it is the devil, bending to his command, who enacts these supernatural deeds. First, these dark entities possess the ability to transport objects with a speed that defies comprehension, flitting from one shadowy corner of the earth to another with eerie swiftness. Such is their dominion over all things lesser, whether born of nature or forged by man. Their agility is terrifying, allowing them to traverse vast distances in the blink of an eye, leaving only a cold whisper in their wake.

Secondly, the demons' knowledge of the natural world is terrifyingly profound. They manipulate the hidden forces of nature with ease, accelerating their effects to bewildering degrees.

Their understanding spans the depths of the mineral, vegetable, and animal realms. With this dark wisdom, they conjure trees, fruits, and beasts in the mere blink of an eye, mocking the natural order. Their unholy ministrations can even cure ailments, either by administering arcane remedies or by possessing the afflicted, driving out malevolent humors from within.

Thirdly, and perhaps most dreadfully, these fiends wield their power over human senses, crafting illusions that ensnare the mind. The pacts forged between these infernal beings and magicians are sealed with dreadful oaths. The sorcerer pledges unwavering obedience to his demonic master, and in return, the demon swears to perform his dark bidding. These unholy alliances are often formalized with ghastly pomp, the demon enthroned in a sepulchral court, surrounded by a legion of spectral attendants and fiendish witnesses."

Thus, the epic struggle between light and dark continues, a chilling reminder of the ever-present shadows lurking just beyond the edge of our sight, waiting for the unwary to stumble and fall into their cold embrace.

In the shadowed realms of the unseen, Swedenborg's soul trembled with a conviction profound and unsettling. He believed, fervently, that certain chosen souls in this life could pierce the veil, communing with spirits from ethereal and infernal realms. Until his death in 1772, he claimed communion with beings of celestial origin and souls of the deceased, narrating tales of otherworldly wonders and horrors, especially those of the infernal regions.

In the annals of time, whispers of spirits haunting the earth abound. Consider the eerie tale of Marcus Brutus, one of Julius Caesar's assassins. On a night shrouded in darkness, within his lonely tent, a monstrous figure emerged at the witching hour. Brutus, heart pounding, demanded, "What art thou, a man or a god? Why art thou here?" The specter, its voice a chilling whisper, replied, "I am thy evil genius; thou shalt see me at Philippi." With a facade of calm, Brutus answered, "I will meet thee there." Yet his body trembled, and his mind was tormented. He recounted the encounter to Cassius, who dismissed it as mere fantasy. Cassius, a follower of Epicurus, scoffed at the notion of spirits, asserting that even if they did exist, they could not take human form or wield power over mortals. Despite Cassius's skepticism, Brutus's unease lingered. Amidst the chaos of the Battle of Philippi, Brutus's vision blurred as he beheld Caesar, spectral and vengeful, charging at him. Overwhelmed by terror, Brutus fell upon his own sword. Cassius, too, met his end by the hand of his freedman, Pindarus.

Pausanius recounts that four hundred years after the Battle of Marathon, the site echoed with ghostly horse neighs and the spectral shouts of soldiers, urging each other to battle. Plutarch describes similar hauntings in the public baths of Chaeronea, his hometown, where murdered citizens' ghosts were seen and dreadful howls heard. These hauntings forced the baths' closure, yet the spectral disturbances persisted, terrifying the neighbors. Plutarch often mentions these apparitions, particularly the ghost of Theseus, who was said to have fought for the Greeks against the Persians.

In the writings of Socrates, it is told that after the Athenian army's defeat under Praetor Laches, as he fled with the Athenian general, he reached a crossroads. He refused to take the same path as the others, explaining that his familiar spirit, a guiding genius, warned him against it. The dire prediction came true, as all who chose the other path were slaughtered or captured by enemy cavalry.

Consider the foreboding tale of Bruno, Archbishop of Würzburg. Shortly before his sudden demise, while sailing with Henry III, he beheld a terrifying specter standing upon a cliff, its eyes burning with malice. The specter hailed him, "Ho! Bishop, I am thy evil genius. Go where thou wilt, thou art and shalt be mine. I am not yet summoned for thee, but soon, thou shalt see me again." The dark waters roiled beneath them, and Bruno's fate was sealed by the chilling prophecy, a shadow that loomed ever closer.

In the ancient city of Athens, a foreboding presence lurked within the walls of a decrepit house. This spirit, a restless and tormented soul, would traverse the darkened halls each night, its movement heralded by the ominous clank of chains. The philosopher Athenodorus, with a heart steeled by curiosity and determination, took residence in this accursed abode, resolute in his quest to unveil the source of the terror that had gripped its inhabitants. One fateful night, as he delved into his scholarly pursuits, the chilling sound of chains disrupted his concentration. Raising his gaze, he was met with the ghastly sight of a spectre materializing before him, its hollow eyes fixed upon him with an otherworldly intensity. The apparition beckoned him with a spectral hand, compelling him to follow. With a mix of dread and resolve, Athenodorus trailed the ghostly figure through the shadowy corridors and into the desolate courtyard. There, the spectre vanished into the earth. The next day, Athenodorus commanded a search of the spot, revealing the shackled skeleton of a long-forgotten soul. The remains were exhumed and given a pyre, their ashes carried away by the wind, and the house, now free of its spectral tormentor, fell silent once more.

In a time shrouded in mystery, a lady embarked on a lonely path under the pale glow of twilight, driven by a desperate need to visit a gravely ill child. As she treaded through the oppressive gloom, her heart pounded with unease. Suddenly, a ghastly vision materialized before her eyes—a spectral form, eerily resembling her friend's child, swathed in a ghostly shroud and ascending towards the heavens. The apparition's silent ascent filled her with a profound dread, and at that very hour, the child's frail life flickered out, succumbing to the cold embrace of death.

Years passed, and aboard a mighty warship off the treacherous coast of Africa, an officer stood vigilant in the inky blackness of night. An inexplicable sense of foreboding gripped him, rendering him paralyzed and unable to rouse himself from his stupor. As the icy fingers of dread closed around him, a cold hand brushed against his skin, jolting him back to awareness. Before him stood a ghostly figure, its pallid form barely distinguishable against the darkened sea. The spectre turned, revealing a familiar visage—the face of his brother, who resided far away in England. The ghost lingered for a few agonizing seconds, its mournful eyes locking with the officer's, before dissolving into the night. Upon his return to Britain, the officer learned of his brother's death, which had occurred at the precise moment he had encountered the spectral vision.

These tales, steeped in the eerie and the epic, remind us that the boundary between the living and the dead is a fragile veil, easily pierced by forces beyond our understanding.

In the annals of lore, whispered tales emerged some two decades past in the untamed reaches of

New South Wales. It was then that the spectral saga first unfolded—a chilling specter, the apparition of a murdered soul haunting the land. The protagonist of this grim tale was none other than Fisher, a stalwart farmer of considerable wealth, yet tragically cut down in his prime, leaving behind a legacy worth £4000.

Whispers drifted amidst the settlers, veiled in uncertainty until a neighbor, the enigmatic Smith, asserted Fisher's departure for distant England, claiming authority over his earthly affairs during absence. Such claims were initially embraced as truth by the community, until a peculiar twist of fate altered the course of belief. It was the elderly Ben Weir, a modest farmer dwelling nearby, whose fateful journey home from Sydney bore witness to a harrowing sight. There, amidst the dim shadows of night, he beheld Fisher's form, visage marred by a grievous wound upon his brow, blood trickling forth in rivulets.

As Weir drew near, the figure vanished into the ether, leaving him bewildered and haunted by the portentous encounter. Fearful of ridicule, he dared not utter a word of what transpired, lest accusations of drunkenness tarnish his name. Yet fate conspired to unveil the truth, for on subsequent nights, the apparition returned, each time beckoning with silent insistence from the very spot where Fisher met his untimely end.

Unable to endure the spectral torment in silence, Weir sought solace in the halls of justice, divulging his unsettling tale to a skeptical magistrate. Initially met with incredulity, his persistence compelled an investigation. Lo, traces of crimson were uncovered at the haunting ground, and not far hence, submerged within a stagnant pond, lay Fisher's lifeless form, a victim of treachery most foul.

Smith, the purported steward of Fisher's estate, stood accused and brought forth to face judgment under the stern gaze of Sir Francis Forbes. His guilt, laid bare by damning evidence and a confession wrung from the clutches of impending doom, sealed his fate. Before the hangman's noose claimed him, Smith's whispered admissions echoed through the hallowed halls—a tale of betrayal and murder, spun amidst the spectral dance of avenging apparitions that prowled the darkened plains of New South Wales.

In the ancient annals of Bow, there stands a tale of dread and haunting that befell a grand house in a bygone century. It began with a maiden's chilling declaration at dawn—the spectral touch of a cold hand had visited her in the midnight hour. Swiftly thereafter, she succumbed to illness, shrouded in death's embrace before the setting of many suns.

Thus commenced a saga of eerie vexations that birthed whispers of a haunted abode. Such terror seized the inhabitants that they forsook the upper and lower chambers, retreating to a lone sanctum on the ground floor. Through day and night, unearthly clamors echoed, as furniture and objects were hurled about by invisible hands.

A valiant gentleman, a friend to the besieged family, took upon himself the task of unraveling the mystery. Venturing into an upper room, he beheld the surreal spectacle: furniture writhing across the floor in a macabre ballet, while unseen forces pelted him with stones and shattered crockery. Every nook and cranny was scrutinized, yet no mortal agency could be found to account for the chaos unleashed.

Fearing the malevolence of otherworldly spirits, he hastened to depart, slamming the door behind him. But it swung open as if by phantom will, and chairs, stools, candlesticks, and plates hurtled after him. Yet, the true horror had not yet unfurled—amidst the stunned onlookers, a pot of boiling water traversed the hearth, poker and tongs exchanged places of their own volition, and pots and pans clashed in a cacophony. A small table levitated in the air, defying reason and sanity.

Whispers of a witch dwelling nearby added a sinister layer to the unfolding drama. A renowned wizard was summoned to confront the malevolent specter, decreeing the fiery fate of the dancing staff. As flames consumed the wood, the suspected witch appeared, writhing in agony and parched with an unquenchable thirst. Suspicion fell heavily upon her, though she evaded conviction for lack of damning proof. Her muttered vow upon departure— "I shall be revenged" — rang ominously in the ears of all who heard.

True to her sinister promise, the night following her release saw a resurgence of torment with redoubled ferocity. The hapless household endured invisible assailants striking with ghostly force, mocking their victims with each blow, while furniture crashed against walls, splintering into shards. With hearts gripped by terror, they fled for their lives, leaving the accursed house to the mercy of the unknown.

In another time and place, upon the dark expanse of the restless sea, a young mariner was roused from slumber by a vision most dire. Before him stood the apparition of his mother, bearing urgent tidings of family matters. Paralyzed with fear, he could but listen as she delivered her message, her form ethereal and her words haunting.

With the message conveyed, the spectral figure retreated slowly, vanishing over the ship's railing to descend gracefully into the depths below. On his return to shore, he learned of his mother's passing at the very hour he had glimpsed her phantom. More bewildering still, the message she imparted to him mirrored that of her ghostly counterpart.

On a subsequent voyage, amidst tales of the seas, the young man recounted to his shipmates the apparition of his mother beckoning to him from the watery abyss—a siren's call amidst tempestuous waters. Fate, however, conspired against him; a raging storm arose, and amidst the chaos, he was swept away into the unforgiving sea. His final words upon the winds, "Mother, I come," lost to the tumultuous night.

Thus concludes these tales of eerie happenings and spectral visitations, where mortal and unearthly realms converge in a dance of dread and destiny.

THE PHANTOM PROPHECY

In the annals of mortal history, scribes of supposed wisdom once whispered that spiritualism was a feeble communion with the unseen, birthed amid the wilds of America in the year 1848. Yet, their musings falter in the face of ancient truths. Long ere Columbus set sail, ere Swedenborg's ink touched paper, spiritualism cast its shadowy veil across the tapestries of Scotland, England, Ireland, and the far reaches of Europe. It was enshrined in the primal beliefs of humanity, long before memory's grasp.

Reginald Scot, in defiance of darkness, penned words against witchcraft and demons in 1584. His tomes, scorned and feared, were consigned to the flames by decree of the gallows' hangman. Yet, in the faded parchments and the murmured verses, the spirit world persisted, unyielding to the whims of men.

In Leipzig, a keeper of coffees and secrets, known as Schrepfer, delved into the forbidden arts of magic. His sorcery, a whispered lore of summoning spirits at will, became his twilight song. Betrayed by insult, he vanished from Leipzig's gaze, only to reappear in Dresden, where princely curiosity sought his darkened arts.

Prince Charles of Saxony, once the architect of Schrepfer's exile, now humbled himself before the sorcerer's might. In a grand display within Dresden's stony halls, Schrepfer commanded the elements unseen. With arcane rites and shrouded invocations, he beckoned forth the specter of Marshal Saxe, uncle to the prince, and harbinger of buried fortunes.

Under the weight of his craft, the room trembled in spectral dance. The air thickened with portent, sweat beading upon Schrepfer's brow like dew upon a grave. From realms beyond, voices echoed—some benevolent, some dire—as the veil between worlds thinned.

Amidst whispers of incantations, a door flung wide, and a shadowy orb rolled forth—a nexus of smoke and faces long forgotten. In thunderous voice, the apparition demanded reckoning, unsettling the bravest hearts of Saxony's court. Prince Charles, in trembling supplication, dared not speak of hidden wealth, nor did the phantom disclose.

With bated breath and lingering fear, the prince implored Schrepfer to dispel the phantom, a plea that strained even the sorcerer's will. Exorcisms echoed into the void, each word a battle against the unseen tide, until at last, the specter receded—only to return, relentless in its hauntings.

Terror seized the gathering, for mortal minds faltered in the presence of the ineffable. Yet Schrepfer, undaunted by mortal trepidation, persisted in his arcane warfare. His name, borne on the lips of Dresden's elite, heralded his prowess over the esoteric.

Under the canopy of Leipzig's verdant glades, seekers of the forbidden convened to witness Schrepfer's final conjuration. In that fateful night, as stars watched in silent witness, the sorcerer retreated to a secluded grove, seeking communion with the abyss.

A gunshot shattered the stillness, reverberating through ancient boughs. His disciples, drawn by awe and dread, found Schrepfer fallen—his heart pierced by unseen hand or treacherous pact. Whispers rose amongst the superstitious, some claiming a pact fulfilled, others a devil's due.

Thus concluded the tale of Schrepfer, whether by mortal hand or infernal design, his fate entwined with shadows darker than mortal coil. The echoes of his sorcery lingered, a cautionary tale for those who dared ply the realms beyond. And in the dimming embers of his legacy, Dresden and Leipzig whispered of a man who danced with spirits and paid the ultimate price.

In the ancient realm of Immola, ruled by Ludovicus Adolisius, a dark prophecy unfurled its shadowed wings. One fateful day, as one of his trusted secretaries journeyed to Ferrara, he encountered a spectral huntsman astride a steed, a falcon poised menacingly on his gloved hand. This apparition, none other than the specter of Ludovicus's own father, spoke with an otherworldly voice, commanding the secretary to summon his lord to a desolate rendezvous at the same hour on the morrow. There, he promised revelations of dire import concerning Immola and its lord.

Shaken to the core by this eerie encounter, the secretary hurried back to Immola to relay the haunting message. Ludovicus, sensing an impending doom, dispatched a subordinate to confront the spectral huntsman. True to the prophecy, the ghostly figure appeared once more, lamenting the lord's absence and forewarning of imminent loss. "In twenty-two years, one month, and one day," it intoned with spectral clarity, "you shall forfeit dominion over the city." Like a fleeting mist, the specter vanished, leaving a chill in its wake.

As prophesied, two decades hence, Philip, Duke of Milan, besieged Immola. With the moat frozen by an uncommon frost, he breached the walls and seized Ludovicus, casting him into captivity.

In another corner of the realm, amidst the intrigue-laden streets of Ferrara, a low-born Italian named Carlo Stella wove his deceitful web. Gaining the favor of Baron Cattaneo, Stella goaded the nobleman into a perilous game of chance, staking not mere gold, but the baron's very ancestral lands. Fortune frowned upon the baron, who, in his defeat and inebriation, unwittingly signed away all he owned to the cunning Stella.

With the dawn of realization, the baron sought to undo his ruinous mistake, only to find Stella brazenly claiming the signed deed as irretrievably destroyed. Days later, tragedy struck when the baron was discovered dead, a bullet piercing his once noble brow. Stella, now armed with the purportedly lost deed, ascended to opulent heights, holding sway over vast riches and ancient fortresses.

Elevated by ill-gotten gains, Stella sought to cement his newfound status by seeking a union with a lady of noble lineage. Amidst a grand ceremony in a hallowed church, as vows were poised to bind, a figure drenched in blood strode forth, fixing Stella with a chilling gaze before vanishing into the night. The ominous interruption shattered the joyous occasion, leaving all in a pall of dread.

Undeterred, Stella pressed for a second ceremony, only to be thwarted once more by supernatural interference. This time, as the moon's pale light struggled against ominous clouds, the bloodied apparition returned, whispering a dire message into Stella's ear before fading once more into darkness. The nuptials were indefinitely postponed, and ultimately canceled by the bride and her kin.

Haunted by guilt and the relentless specter,

Stella's nights became tortured by phantoms and spectral wails. Consumed by remorse, he turned to dark arts and sought out a feared witch, known for communing with the spirits of the departed. Through her arcane rituals and sacrificial gold, the witch summoned the vengeful spirit of Baron Cattaneo, binding it in a fiery circle of conjured flames. Despite fierce resistance, the ghostly avenger foretold a reckoning: "Murderer, we shall soon meet again," it hissed before vanishing back into the abyss.

Tormented and driven to madness, Stella spiraled into a maelstrom of despair. In his fevered delirium, he sought solace in drink and frenzied flights through the night, pursued by unseen horrors. Witnesses feared the worst as he careened towards a precipitous fate.

On a fateful day, his steed thundered relentlessly towards a treacherous bridge over a roiling river. Spurred on by frantic desperation, Stella and his mount hurtled over the edge, vanishing into the churning waters below. Thus ended the tale of

Carlo Stella, consumed by the infernal depths, his tormented soul forever entwined with the dark echoes of his misdeeds.

THE SPECTRAL LEGACY

In the days when Henry VIII ruled the land, a tale of dark portent reached the ears of Mr. Gresham, a merchant of London. Returning from Palermo, where Antonio the Rich held sway over vast dominions, Mr. Gresham encountered a chilling prophecy that echoed through his soul. Antonio, infamous for his wealth amassed through dubious means, was said to wield power beyond mortal understanding. His riches were gained through usury and tyranny, a hoard that seemed to defy the heavens themselves.

During an unexpected delay at Strombuli, where fierce winds held them captive, Mr. Gresham and his crew ventured to the fiery heart of a volcano.

As they approached the seething crater, a voice bellowed forth from the depths, proclaiming, "Haste, haste! The rich Antonio draws near!" Fear gripped their hearts as they hurried down the mountain, just in time to witness flames erupt in a violent display.

Upon arriving in Palermo, Mr. Gresham sought out Antonio, only to learn that the man had perished precisely at the moment the infernal voice had foretold his coming. This uncanny revelation shook Mr. Gresham to his core, and upon his return to England, he recounted the eerie events to King Henry VIII. The sailors swore to the truth of their harrowing experience.

Haunted by the specter of Antonio's fate, Mr. Gresham renounced his mercantile pursuits, bestowing his wealth generously upon the needy and committing his days to righteous deeds. Thus, in the shadow of a prophecy fulfilled, Mr. Gresham's legacy was not of riches, but of virtue and the lingering chill of a tale that defied reason and dared to peer into the abyss.

In the ancient city of Königsberg, a revered scholar of moral philosophy once embarked on a journey that would plunge him into the depths of both history and horror. Bestowed by the Prussian monarch, William I, with a humble benefice nestled deep in the heart of the countryside, far from the bustling streets of Königsberg, the young professor took possession of the quaint parsonage. Little did he know that within those aged walls, a chilling tale awaited.

Upon settling into the parsonage, he chose to reside in the very room where his predecessor, now departed from the mortal realm, had once laid his head to rest. It was here, as the veil of night began to lift, that the professor's world was forever altered. The somber silence was shattered by the rustling of unseen pages, emanating from a spectral figure clad in a flowing gown. Standing before a lectern adorned with an imposing tome, the apparition's pallid visage bore the weight of profound sorrow. Beside him stood two young boys, their innocent faces reflecting the solemnity of the scene.

With deliberate steps, the ghostly figure closed the ancient book and, grasping each child gently by the hand, glided solemnly across the room. They vanished behind an iron stove that loomed ominously in the chamber's darkest corner. Overwhelmed by the spectral encounter, the young parson kept his harrowing experience cloaked in secrecy, pondering the meaning of this eerie visitation.

In the Lutheran tradition of Prussian churches, it was customary to commemorate past pastors with solemn portraits. Moved by an inexplicable urge, the professor ventured to examine these relics of the past. There, amidst the rows of framed visages, he stumbled upon a portrait that struck him with a chilling recognition—the very likeness of the spectral figure that had haunted his chamber.

His curiosity piqued, the professor sought out the church's sexton, a custodian of local lore and whispers that lingered in the folds of time. In hushed tones, the sexton revealed fragments of a tragic tale—the departed pastor, revered for his wisdom and kindness, had met an untimely end, whispered to be caused by a heart rent asunder by anguish.

Digging deeper into the shadows of history, the professor learned of scandalous whispers that tainted the late pastor's memory—a forbidden liaison with a local woman, shrouded in secrets and the birth of two sons. The same sons whose spectral forms had materialized in his bedchamber, only to vanish mysteriously before their supposed father's demise.

As winter's icy grip tightened its hold, practical matters demanded the professor's attention. Faced with the challenge of warming the very room where ghostly figures had once roamed, he sought the aid of a skilled tradesman. Together, they probed the depths of the stubborn stove, uncovering a grim truth that sent shivers down their spines—the bones of two small children, nestled deep within the stove's bowels. These remains, small and fragile, bore a haunting resemblance to the spectral children he had glimpsed.

Thus, the professor's journey into the unknown unfolded, weaving together threads of the past and present in a tapestry of eerie revelations. In the depths of that remote parsonage, where history whispered through the cracks of time, the veil between the living and the dead was torn asunder, revealing secrets that echoed through the ages.

In the twilight of his days, Mozart, the renowned maestro of melodies, harbored an unyielding dread of death, a relentless specter that haunted his every moment. His soul, cloaked in melancholy, was enshrouded with a foreboding darkness that foretold of an impending fate.

Legend tells of a fateful encounter that would mark his final opus. On a day when despair weighed heavily upon him, a figure of imposing stature and grave countenance materialized—a harbinger from the shadowed realms beyond. This stranger, draped in mystery, beseeched Mozart to craft a requiem of solemn grandeur, a testament to a departed soul dear to his heart. With solemn eyes that seemed to pierce into the depths of eternity, the stranger commissioned the piece, offering a substantial sum of a hundred ducats as earnest.

Mozart, gripped by an otherworldly compulsion, accepted the task, pledging completion within a month's time. Yet, as he delved into the ethereal strains of the requiem, he sensed an uncanny prescience—a whisper from the void that this composition was not merely for another, but for himself. "This requiem," he declared with a solemn tremor, "is my own, a solemn echo of my farewell."

Days turned to nights as Mozart immersed himself in feverish creation, his body faltering under the strain, yet his spirit ablaze with an eerie determination. Fainting fits and failing health beset him, yet he pressed on, driven by an unseen force compelling him to finish what fate had ordained.

When the month's end approached, the enigmatic stranger returned as promised, but Mozart had transcended mortal bounds. His requiem, however, stood complete, a haunting testament woven from the fabric of his final days. The stranger, undeterred by the absence of the composer, acknowledged the extended labor and increased the promised bounty by fifty ducats, a gesture that echoed with cryptic significance.

As whispers spread of the mysterious visitor's origins, Mozart's servants sought to unveil the truth, only to find themselves thwarted by the veil of night that enveloped the stranger's departure. In the end, Mozart's conviction remained steadfast: the stranger had been a harbinger, a messenger from realms beyond, sent to beckon him towards his inevitable journey.

Thus, amidst the whispers of an unfinished requiem, Mozart's legacy echoed through the corridors of time—a haunting melody that spoke of mortality and the ceaseless dance with destiny.

In the dim annals of history, amidst the echoes of forgotten kingdoms, there dwells the spectral tale of a forlorn lady whose sorrow spans the ages. It is said that in the fifteenth century, she succumbed to the cruel machinations of her husband, yet her spirit, bound by anguish, traversed beyond mortal confines. Known as "the White Lady," her form clad in spectral white, she roamed the ancestral halls of Brandenburg, Baden, and Darmstadt, and ventured to distant realms unknown.

Her presence, a harbinger of impending fate, haunted the corridors of castles and palaces alike. Through ethereal veils, a faint luminescence pierced, casting eerie shadows upon her path. Wherever she appeared, whispers of imminent demise swirled like mist in her wake. The residents of these ancient keeps knew: the spectral visitation foretold the passing of one bound to the house by blood or kinship.

In lands afar, another manifestation of the White Lady revealed itself. Through moonlit panes, she peered into the chambers where souls prepared to depart from earthly shores. A silent sentinel of the threshold between life and beyond, her visage struck dread into those who beheld her countenance in the moments of finality.

Yet in yet another realm, whispers spoke of a spectral form that hovered amidst the heavens, a guardian of those who crossed the veil. Her ethereal form, bathed in the pallor of twilight, bore witness to the souls bidding farewell to mortal coils.

Thus, across realms and ages, the legend of the White Lady endures—a testament to the boundary between the known and the supernatural, where the epic and the eerie intertwine, weaving tales of sorrow and transcendence through the tapestry of time itself.

In the dawn of the first upheaval of the French Revolution, Lady Pennyman and her kin withdrew to Lisle, where they secured a vast manor for a meager fee. In the midst of their sojourn within this edifice, Lady Pennyman received from her spouse, Sir John Pennyman, a warrant for a princely sum, which she conveyed to a local banker, demanding its conversion into cash. Much of the amount was disbursed in silver, and, with various errands yet to attend, she tasked the banker to dispatch the funds to her residence in a parcel. This package was entrusted to a porter; when the lady inquired if he comprehended the directions to the intended abode, he assured her he knew it well—it was known as the "Haunted House." She scarcely pondered his words at the time, but soon they returned to her mind in a manner that startled her profoundly.

The household steward approached Lady Pennyman weeks later, revealing that two servants, who had journeyed with her from England, had given notice that very morning. They cited nightly terror induced by spectral voices haunting their chambers. This revelation stirred Lady Pennyman, a woman of steely resolve who scoffed at tales of ghosts and haunted dwellings. To convince her retainers to stay, she resolved to sleep in a room recently vacated by one of the departed servants. Here, she discovered a large iron cage, and the chilling tale that accompanied it. It was whispered that a former owner, a wealthy youth, had been confined within by his guardian uncle during his youth, subjected to starvation and cruel torment until his untimely demise.

For several nights, all seemed calm, and Lady Pennyman dared to hope that peace would return to her domain. But her hopes were dashed. One fateful night, she was roused by footsteps echoing in the notorious "cage chamber." Meanwhile, her son, recently returned from the sea, was plagued by incessant knocking at his door and apparitions that defied explanation. Determined to unravel the mystery, a friend volunteered to spend the night in the "cage room," accompanied only by a loyal hound.

Locked securely inside, he settled in for the vigil, confident in his fortitude. Yet his confidence was short-lived. Before long, his canine companion, usually fearless, leapt into bed, whimpering and terrified. The chamber door creaked open slowly, admitting a spectral figure—a pallid, frail youth who approached the iron cage, leaned against its bars for a fleeting moment, then vanished as mysteriously as he had appeared. Undeterred, the gentleman pursued the ghostly apparition. Upon reaching the door, he found it firmly locked from the inside, just as he had left it. His resolve undiminished, he followed the specter down the stairs, witnessing its gradual descent until it dissolved into the earth below.

The revelation of this unearthly visitation spread like wildfire, plunging the household into panic. Ultimately, Lady Pennyman and her kin abruptly departed the accursed abode, leaving behind a legacy of dread and the unanswered question: who—or what—haunted the "cage chamber"?

In the annals of history, the tale of the celebrated Duchess of Mazarin and Madame de Beauclair resonates with eerie splendor. These two illustrious women, favored by kings and steeped in mystery, shared an uncommon bond. They dwelled in opulent chambers within Stable Yard, St. James's, yet withdrew from the world, veiled in secrets known only to themselves.

A pact, born of whispered promises, bound them together: that the first to depart for the realm beyond would return, breaching the divide between life and death to recount its mysteries. This solemn vow echoed through the years until fate intervened. The Duchess of Mazarin, gravely ill, stood on the precipice of eternity. As Madame de Beauclair gently reminded her of their pact, the duchess, with steadfast resolve, assured her friend that their covenant would be fulfilled.

Upon the duchess's passing, silence reigned. Years turned into a void of unanswered prayers until one fateful eve when the veil between worlds thinned. Madame de Beauclair, seated in solitude, beheld a specter emerging from the shadows—an apparition of the Duchess of Mazarin. Gliding with ethereal grace, the ghostly figure approached and spoke with haunting sweetness: "Beauclair, between the hours of twelve and one this night, you will be with me."

Such words pierced the veil of disbelief that shrouded Madame de Beauclair's heart. Though robust in health, a foreboding certainty gripped her soul. She summoned her confidants, imparted final tokens of affection, and sought solace in spiritual counsel. Skeptics sought to dissuade her, dismissing her visions as fevered delusions. Yet, resolute, she declared, "My eyes and ears have not deceived me. The Duchess of Mazarin has spoken truth."

As midnight approached, she appeared unchanged, defying all logic. But within her, a storm raged, unseen and inexorable. "I am already sick at heart," she lamented, her countenance betraying the turmoil within. Before the tolling of the hour, Madame de Beauclair succumbed, departing the mortal realm as foretold.

Thus, in the grand tapestry of their friendship, woven with threads of courtly intrigue and spectral prophecy, the Duchess of Mazarin and

Madame de Beauclair transcended the boundaries of mortality, leaving a legacy intertwined with the whispers of the beyond.

THE HAUNTING PROPHECY

In the annals of Windsor Castle, during the dawning of the seventeenth century, a young officer in service to the king found himself the subject of extraordinary visitations. These spectral encounters, shrouded in eerie luminescence, began with the manifestation of a figure that spoke with the voice of the departed Sir George Villiers. This ethereal messenger bore grave tidings for the officer: a prophecy of doom unless a message was delivered to Sir George's son, the illustrious Duke of Buckingham.

Night after night, the ghostly form returned, its presence growing more ominous with each appearance. The officer, initially hesitant, soon felt the weight of unfulfilled promises as the apparition's warnings intensified. In a vision of unsettling grandeur, the spirit vowed dire consequences should its commands remain unheeded.

Driven by fear and a sense of impending destiny, the officer journeyed swiftly to London, the seat of power, seeking an audience with Sir Ralph Freeman. Together, they orchestrated a clandestine meeting with the Duke of Buckingham, arranged on the banks of Lambeth Bridge before the break of dawn. There, under the cloak of mist and secrecy, words were exchanged that moved the Duke profoundly, his emotions tumultuous beneath a stoic façade.

The Duke's countenance betrayed turmoil upon his return from the hunt, and though he received further omens of impending tragedy, he chose to dismiss them. Yet fate, like an inexorable shadow, loomed ever closer. On a fateful day in August 1628, the Duke of Buckingham met his end at the hand of John Felton, a disgruntled lieutenant at

Portsmouth. The news of his demise reached his mother, who, in her grief, acknowledged the prescience of the apparitions she had long believed in.

Thus, the tale of the officer's spectral warnings and the Duke's tragic fate echoed through the corridors of Windsor Castle, a testament to the chilling intersection of prophecy and mortal ambition in the epic saga of the Villiers dynasty.

In the depths of winter in 1778, Lord Lyttelton departed the bustling metropolis, accompanied by a retinue of debauched companions, intent on profaning Christmas with their riotous revelries at his country estate near Epsom. As they surrendered themselves to reckless indulgence, a sudden pall descended upon the gathering as their host, usually full of mirth and vigor, grew unnaturally despondent and withdrew from their midst.

Pressed to divulge the cause of his distress, Lord Lyttelton recounted a chilling encounter. He spoke of retiring to his chambers the previous night, whereupon, with his lamp extinguished, he heard a fluttering outside his window. Peering into the darkness, he beheld the spectral form of a tormented woman—whom he had wronged and who had taken her own life—standing in silent accusation. Approaching his bedside, she pointed an ethereal finger towards a clock on the mantelpiece, foretelling that unless he repented, his life and transgressions would cease at the hour of the third day hence.

In an otherworldly luminescence that suffused the chamber, he witnessed every detail with eerie clarity as the apparition delivered its ominous message precisely at midnight. Though his companions scoffed at his terror, attributing it to a fevered dream, Lord Lyttelton remained unsettled, haunted by the specter's warning.

As the fateful hour approached, Lord Lyttelton's servants, in collusion with his guests, surreptitiously advanced the clocks by an hour and a half. They endeavored to distract their lord with lively diversions, yet as the night wore on, a leaden silence fell upon him. At the stroke of ten, his mood grew somber; at eleven, it deepened further; and when the clock tolled twelve, he breathed a sigh of relief, declaring triumphantly that the ghost had deceived him, and he was safe from harm.

Yet unbeknownst to him, the ominous hour had not yet passed. Ignorant of the ruse, he retired to his chamber, bidding his guests goodnight in false assurance. Meanwhile, his companions, despite their professed disbelief, remained together in fearful vigilance. The valet's descent from Lord Lyttelton's room punctuated the stillness—a mere instant before the tolling of midnight. The tolling of the bell summoned them to his bedside, where they discovered their noble host, life extinguished, his visage contorted in a ghastly grimace.

Thus concluded the tale of Lord Lyttelton—a saga of revelry turned sinister, where the boundary between the living and the spectral dissolved in a crescendo of foreboding and dread.

In the twilight hours preceding the passing of an

ancient Roman sovereign, the realm was besieged by omens both ominous and awe-inspiring. As the king languished in illness, a tempest of unprecedented fury swept through the city, tearing down the holy symbol atop a revered church. Following this cataclysm, the very earth convulsed in a violent earthquake, its tremors shaking the very foundations of the imperial capital.

Amidst this turmoil, an aged eagle, long a denizen of the royal precincts, abruptly took flight, vanishing into the obscurity of the unknown. Simultaneously, the bells of the imperial chapel tolled a haunting melody thrice in the span of a mere twelve hours, their mournful peals echoing through the corridors of power.

But the most chilling of all portents unfolded under the shroud of midnight. Shadows danced unnaturally across the palace courtyard, while spectral figures materialized in the air above and skulked amongst the palace halls. Most unsettling of all was the spectral procession witnessed one fateful night: a funeral cortege of ghostly apparitions, winding its way solemnly from the heart of the palace to the royal sepulcher, where soon the mortal remains of the monarch would find eternal rest.

Thus, as the king lay on the brink of eternity, the world around him trembled with foreboding, heralding the end of an epoch with the eerie whispers of fate.

In the ancient chronicles of the Eddas, tales echo of a time when the boundary between the living and the dead was thin, where ghosts, spirits, and demons roamed in shadowed forms. Among these chronicles, let us unveil a saga of spectres woven with threads of the eerie and the profound.

When Helge, the warrior of the North, met his end, his spirit did not rest. A maiden, under the veiled twilight sky, beheld his ghostly retinue as they rode silently into the barrow where Helge's earthly vessel lay entombed. The maiden dared to question the apparition's reality, only to receive a chilling affirmation from the ethereal host. Swiftly, she bore the haunting news to Sigrum, Helge's bereaved widow, whose heart still bled with grief.

Sigrum, with steadfast resolve, hastened to the mound and there, amidst the shadows of the dead, she encountered the spectral form of her beloved. His ghostly voice resonated with lament and longing, speaking words that pierced the silence of the tomb. "Sigrum, you are the reason I lie here, slain by the sorrowful dew. Your tears, like fire, burn bright, yet we shall share the mead of the gods, though joy and lands are lost. Here we lie, with brides in barrows and princely maidens by our side."

Moved by a love that transcended death, Sigrum fashioned a bed within the cairn and beckoned the ghost to find solace from eternal unrest. "Son of the Ylfinga," she spoke softly, "rest here with me, as once you did in life." The ghost, touched by her devotion, whispered in reply, "No longer do I doubt your faithfulness, for you offer solace in death's embrace. Though you live, offspring of kings, let the pale steed tread the skies, for we must journey westward, to the bridge Vindhjalen, before the cock crows in Walhalla and awakens the victors."

Thus, amidst the twilight of the gods and the echoes of forgotten battles, the saga of Helge and Sigrum resonates—an epic of love and loss, where the veil between the worlds grows thin, and the spirits of the departed whisper their tales through the ages.

In the distant annals of time, when the echoes of forgotten sorrows still whispered through the wind, there lived a specter—a phantom born of tragedy in the chilling lands of Iceland. This ghostly maiden, forsaken in death, returned from beyond to exact a dire reckoning upon the living who dared defy her dying wishes. Her mortal remains, denied their rightful rest, were borne to a desolate tomb in a far-off place. Yet, fate conspired against her repose, delaying the interment to a fateful eve.

As darkness veiled the world, the bearers sought shelter within a solitary house, oblivious to the sinister specter that awaited. At the stroke of midnight, her ethereal form glided through the cold stone of the kitchen, a harbinger of dread and doom. Henceforth, each night saw her apparition, a luminous crescent in perpetual orbit around the dwelling, a celestial dance that mirrored the sun's descent.

The wise and learned, steeped in ancient lore, beheld this ominous display and proclaimed it a prophecy foretelling pestilence and demise. Demoniacal forces stirred amidst the living, plaguing a herdsman who met his untimely end, tormented by unseen malevolence. Thorer, in his arrogance, dared to interpret these omens, only to meet a grisly fate at the spectral hands of the shepherd's ghost, crushed beneath the weight of spectral vengeance.

Such horrors multiplied as days turned to nights— a poltergeist's wrath overturned tables and sent kitchenware spinning in chaotic frenzy. Even a demon in guise of a seal rose from the earth, spreading terror among the household. Thorodd, master of the estate, met his watery grave along with his servants, condemned to roam his ancestral halls as phantom shades. Yet, amid these terrors, the Christian folk found solace in the belief that these apparitions, perhaps favored by the ancient goddess Rana, sought no ill beyond their spectral hauntings.

But as the demonic horde swelled to thirty, matching the number of those claimed by their wrath, panic gripped the land. Many fled, fearing death's icy grip and the infernal clutches awaiting their souls. Yet, hope flickered in the form of a devout priest, a beacon of divine light amidst encroaching darkness. With holy water and solemn rites, he confronted the malevolent spirits, casting them back into the shadows from whence they came.

Thus, through the priest's exorcism, the land was cleansed of its spectral scourge, banished to the nether realms with vows never to return. And so, the tale of the haunted mansion and its ghastly visitors faded into legend, a cautionary tale etched in the annals of time—a reminder of the fragile veil between the living and the dead, and the eternal struggle against forces unseen.

THE PHANTOM RIDER

In the hallowed annals of Lord Lyttelton's Letters lies a tale shrouded in mystery and dread, whispered by those whose integrity stands unblemished. Behold, the saga unfolds thus:

In the prime of antiquity, amidst the revelry of a hunting fraternity, a figure cloaked in elegance and astride a steed of unearthly vigor joined the pursuit. His prowess knew no bounds, defying the very laws of mortal men. Hounds faltered in their chase; hunters lagged behind, muttering of infernal origins to his equine companion. Yet, when the hunt concluded, the company, captivated by his charisma, bid the stranger to their repast.

At dinner's table, he enthralled all with his discourse, weaving tales of oratory, poetry, art, and law with an otherworldly grace. His words, like tendrils of enchantment, bound the guests in rapt attention, delaying the veil of sleep. As the night waned and guests sought respite, unease crept upon him, compelling him to augment his spellbinding oratory, holding the remaining few in thrall.

But with the witching hour's approach, terror rent the calm. Shrieks, born of damnation itself, tore through the tranquility of the manor. Startled from slumber, guests attributed it to beasts or phantoms confined in shadowed corners. Yet, each cry pierced deeper, till realization dawned— it emanated from the stranger's chamber.

Brave souls, roused by valor or curiosity, ventured forth. Within the sanctum, they found him, knelt upon crimsoned sheets, flagellating his flesh in penance. Bloodied streaks marked his fervor, his voice beseeching mercy, promising explanation at dawn.

Morning light unveiled an empty chamber, stained with remnants of a harrowing night. The stranger, vanished as phantom mist, spurred his mount into oblivion, leaving naught but dread in his wake. Pursuit proved futile, as if he melted into the ether, leaving behind a legend ensconced in the chilling embrace of the unknown.

In the misty reaches of the Scotch Highlands, ancient tales whisper of eerie encounters with beings of darkness and magic. One such legend speaks of witches who, in the guise of hares, faced mortal peril at the jaws of vigilant hounds. These stories, echoing through time, seem but variations of a singular, ominous narrative.

Behold, a rendition unfolds thus: In the hush of dawn, a hunter beheld an old crone skulking through a shadowed glen, her presence stirring suspicion. Intent on unraveling her mystery, he shadowed her stealthy steps until he drew near enough to discern her countenance. She was known to him, a respected neighbor of the glen. Sensing his approach, the crone hastened,

THE BOOK OF DEMONOLOGY

transforming into a hare with uncanny speed. Swiftly she darted away, but the hunter's faithful hound gave chase, and in a flurry of primal struggle, the hare was seized. A haunting shriek pierced the air, reverberating through the hills, as if the very earth recoiled in dread.

Approaching cautiously, the hunter witnessed a raven take flight, its harsh cry a harbinger of ill omen. Amidst a pool of crimson, his loyal hounds lay lifeless. Returning home, he learned the crone lay gravely ill, her life ebbing away. That fateful night, another villager ventured homeward, his path winding through the ancient churchyard and a darkened wood, domains whispered to be favored by spirits foul.

As the moon's gaze dimmed by the forest's embrace, he encountered a woman sprinting toward the church, questioning if she could reach its sanctuary ere the midnight hour. Her voice, her visage—the hunter's memory stirred, for she resembled the crone of the morning. Moments later, he encountered two hounds coursing with preternatural speed, and then a figure cloaked in darkness—a rider astride a steed of ebony. The horseman queried urgently of the woman and her pursuers, eyes aflame with infernal light, while the steed exhaled smoke and fire.

Fear gripped the traveler's heart, his resolve faltering. He hastened homeward, haunted by the dread of the night's horrors. Passing the crone's dwelling, he glimpsed a flickering light and entered, only to learn of her passing. Convinced the figure he had encountered was no mortal, but the spirit of the departed witch, and her pursuers fiends from the nether realms, he departed swiftly, leaving behind a cursed abode.

Yet, as he crossed the threshold, a chilling sight arrested his gaze—the black horseman racing toward the house, the crone draped across his steed, with the hounds close behind. In an instant, horse and riders vanished into the earth's maw, leaving the traveler shaken, his soul chilled by the encounter with forces beyond mortal ken.

THE HAUNTING OF PEST

In the annals of ancient lore and sacred manuscripts, it is recounted that noble men, especially those who led the charge in the venerable Church of old, endured terrifying assaults from the Prince of Darkness himself. Not only did they grapple with unseen legions of shadowy spirits, but they faced the Devil in his corporeal guise, relentless in his quest to lure them from their steadfast faith. None were spared from these relentless confrontations, least of all the revered saints of the ancient Catholic Church, who bore the brunt of diabolic fury.

Yet, to their eternal glory, the champions of the Church almost invariably emerged victorious.

Armed with unshakable righteousness and safeguarded by miraculous relics, the saints defied the adversary of mankind in epic clashes that resonated through the ages. Seekers of deeper knowledge on these harrowing encounters are advised to consult the Chronicles of the Saints and the revered Calendars penned by learned scribes, who chronicled their truths with unyielding conviction. The following chronicles, when read alongside the sacred verses of Chapter XV, substantiate these steadfast truths.

Consider the valor of St. Maurus, who confronted Satan and his infernal cohort manifest in corporeal forms. With but a word of rebuke, Maurus banished the demonic throng, though not before their presence shook the very foundations of the monastery, bringing the devout monks to their knees in fearful reverence.

St. Romualdus endured a five-year ordeal locked in dire combat with Satan himself, appearing in forms visible to mortal eyes. St. Frances possessed the eerie gift of perceiving malevolent spirits unseen by ordinary mortals, revealing their haunting presence amidst natural semblances. St. Gregory bore witness to the chilling spectacle of the Devil entering a man consumed by the love of falsehoods and deceit.

A monk, gripped by the temptation to abandon his sacred vows and renounce his monastic calling, found himself beset by the Devil, taking the menacing guise of a midnight-black hound. Others who dared to break their solemn pledges fared no better, their souls cast into turmoil and divine retribution.

In Rome, a nobleman defied St. Gregory's righteous decree and faced excommunication for his unlawful actions. Seeking vengeance, he consorted with pagan witches and sorcerers, who invoked infernal forces to ensnare the holy Pontiff. They wrought dark enchantments, compelling a steed of the Pope to rear and fling its rider to an untimely end.

Yet, the venerable Gregory, ever vigilant, discerned the treachery and swiftly expelled the

Devil from the possessed steed, striking the sorcerers with a blinding curse. When entreated to restore their sight, he steadfastly refused, lest they be tempted anew by the forbidden arts of sorcery and necromancy.

Thus, in the shadowed tapestry of ages past, these legends echo — tales of valor and spiritual strife, where saints battled the forces of darkness in epic duels that forged the very fabric of faith and righteousness.

In ancient days of yore, the noble St. Benedict faced the tempter in harrowing encounters that shook the very fabric of his devout existence. Once, the devil, cunning in his guile, took form as a little blackbird, its sweet melody weaving a sinister enchantment around the saint. Nearly ensnared from his path of prayer, St. Benedict summoned a power far greater than mortal strength and conquered the adversary. Stripping himself bare, he flung his body upon a thicket of thorns and briars, rending flesh and soul alike until crimson rivers flowed, purging the seductive spell

THE BOOK OF DEMONOLOGY

that sought to lead him astray.

Yet the devil's malice knew no bounds. He dared obstruct the sacred work of monastery walls, and in a fit of wickedness, hurled a stone that claimed the life of a young monk. Undeterred by such evil, St. Benedict, in his divine benevolence, banished the infernal fiend and restored life to the fallen disciple. Vigilant over the spiritual guardianship of his brethren, the saint beheld the devil's dark ride upon a mule, possessing the very soul of an elder monk whose heart harbored covetous desires. Through penance and the sanctity of holy relics, the malevolent spirit was exorcised, and the monk's soul purified.

In another realm of sanctity, St. Francis, beacon of divine servitude, wielded dominion over all creation. Fire, air, water, and earth bent to his sacred will. He repelled wicked spirits, bestowed sight upon the blind, speech upon the mute, health upon the infirm, and even breathed life into the departed. The elements, in awe of his purity, dared not harm him; he walked unscathed upon searing flames, and thrust his hands into blazing ovens without a single blister. With his companion, they traversed the tempestuous sea atop his cloak, which lay serenely upon the tumultuous waves.

Thus, in epic sagas of bravery and righteousness, these holy men walked the path of legends, defying darkness with their unwavering faith and miraculous deeds that echoed through the annals of time.

In the annals of sanctity, St. Catherine, undaunted by the very presence of malevolent spirits, stood resolute against their wicked machinations. Once, as two condemned thieves, their souls laden with sin, faced their fate on the way to execution, a grim procession accompanied them, a cart of torment and despair. While all but the saint saw naught but the physical agony, Catherine beheld a legion of devils, cunning and vile, goading the criminals to blaspheme and curse.

Moved by divine compassion, Catherine stepped into the very chariot of damnation, confronting the spectral horde that swirled around the hapless men. With righteous fury, she banished the infernal tormentors, replacing their taunts with words of repentance and contrition. Thus, through her intercession, the condemned souls found solace in their final moments, their spirits cleansed before meeting justice.

As for St. Stanislaus, his life was a testament to miracles that rivaled the ancient wonders of old. Evil spirits quaked at his approach, dispersing like chaff in the tempest. Diseases yielded to his touch, and even death itself was but a temporary pause in his sacred mission.

In a remarkable display of his celestial power, Stanislaus found himself embroiled in a legal dispute over a parcel of land purchased from a man named Peter. The deceased's heirs, spurred by ill intent and political intrigue, sought to reclaim the land unlawfully. Yet, before the court could decree the unjust ruling, Stanislaus invoked a divine pause, beseeching heaven for three days of respite.

During this interlude, the saint fasted and prayed with fervent dedication. At its end, fortified by the sacrament of the Mass, he ventured to Peter's sepulcher. With a gentle touch of his crosier, he commanded the dead to rise. Astonished witnesses beheld as Peter, roused from the depths of mortality, testified unequivocally to the legality of the transaction. His solemn oath settled the dispute, affirming the rightful ownership of the land, consecrated for the service of the Church.

Peter, though offered a reprieve from the eternal slumber, chose instead to return to the purgatorial fires, where he yet endured the cleansing flames for his earthly transgressions. His steadfast resolve inspired awe among the onlookers, who witnessed the saint escorting Peter back to his resting place. With solemn ceremony, Peter laid himself down in the earth once more, sealing his fate amidst the throngs of the faithful, who bore witness to the divine justice and mercy that flowed through the life of St. Stanislaus.

In the annals of celestial chronicles, the saga of St. Philip Nerius unfolds amidst ethereal visions and encounters with infernal spirits. As he steadfastly discharged his sacred duties, three sinister apparitions dared to cross his path, their dark forms a chilling juxtaposition to the divine radiance that enveloped the saint. Yet even in death, St. Philip Nerius did not depart quietly into the beyond; instead, he manifested to his chosen disciples in a blaze of resplendent light, a testament to his transcendent spirit and unwavering faith.

Across the ages, the venerable St. Erasmus, amidst the clutches of captivity, found solace in spectral voices that shattered his chains and spoke solace to his troubled heart. It was said that spirits ministered unto him, their whispers carrying both dread and divine comfort, forging a legend of fortitude amid spectral trials.

St. Norbert, wielder of divine authority, commanded the very forces of darkness, expelling demons from the souls they tormented. In his era, malevolent spirits roamed freely, baring the sins of mortals until the saint silenced their accusatory tongues, compelling them to secrecy under the sacrament of confession. Even in death, his visage returned to those who held his memory, a spectral beacon of righteous power.

Legend also speaks of Henry I, the emperor, whose final moments drew the attention of cosmic forces. As his soul teetered upon the precipice of eternity, a hermit glimpsed the devil himself racing towards the sovereign's bedchamber, intent upon claiming a soul ripe for the taking. "Whither goest thou?" demanded the hermit of the fiendish intruder. "To witness the monarch's demise," came the chilling reply. Commanded to return with news of his success, the devil swiftly retraced his steps, only to return in anguish and dismay. "We are deceived!" he cried out in despair. "Our schemes are thwarted, our powers undone! Angels have intervened, their scales balanced by a mysterious figure—burnt and yet luminous—who added a weight of righteousness that eclipsed our dark machinations. Victory was proclaimed, and the soul was borne away on celestial wings, leaving us naught but shame and defeat."

This mysterious figure was none other than the venerable St. Lawrence, the martyr whose fiery trial upon the gridiron had transformed him into a beacon of celestial justice, forever confounding the plans of the infernal realm.

Thus, the tapestry of history weaves together these epic and eerie tales, where mortal deeds and celestial interventions converge in a cosmic struggle of light and shadow, faith and damnation.

In the annals of celestial valor and eerie confrontation, St. Margaret once faced a serpent whose very gaze bespoke death itself. Undeterred, she seized victory from the jaws of peril, as she had done in countless battles prior. Though the serpent's venom wounded her deeply and frequently, divine healing bestowed upon her a lasting peace that defied the malice of her adversary.

St. Ignatius, marked by an ominous command over demons, was relentlessly hunted as their most formidable adversary. In the shadowed alleys of Paris and the ancient halls of Rome, the fiends manifested in grotesque forms. They assailed him fiercely, nearly choking the life from him and scourging him with torment that lingered. Yet, through unyielding resilience, he emerged victorious. During his earthly sojourn, the arch-fiend wielded formidable power, possessing innocents and conjuring tempests with unholy fervor. But the saint stood unflinching, facing the abyss itself.

Once, within the walls of a Loretto college, holy men were besieged by demons whose terrifying cacophony and monstrous visages defied all mortal understanding. Prayers and exorcisms faltered until the presence of Father Ignatius was invoked. With effortless grace, he banished the tormentors, as if they were mere trifles, dispersing them like fleeting shadows.

St. Stephen, with an ironclad will, held dominion

over Satan, casting out demons from threescore and thirteen afflicted souls.

St. Dominick, a beacon of righteousness, drew the ire of Satan, who waged relentless war against his soul and body. Yet, a man who commanded the power to resurrect the deceased—such as when St. Donatus summoned forth a woman to reveal hidden treasure—faced the devil undaunted. The saint's miracles exposed falsehoods and brought justice to light.

St. Cyriacus, St. Largus, and St. Smaragdus wrought wonders beyond comprehension, driving malevolent spirits not only from individuals but from entire realms. Cyriacus, renowned across distant kingdoms for his mastery over darkness, was sought by princes to banish demons to their rightful abyss.

St. Clare, a beacon of purity in a turbulent world, engaged in fierce battle with the devil, who assumed a sinister form. Though frail in stature, she wielded divine strength and overcame the darkness that sought to assail her, emerging triumphant in spiritual combat.

In the annals of saints' valor and divine providence, the legends of St. Bernard unfold with eerie magnificence. Armed not with mere faith, but with a sacred crook hewn from the sanctified wood of St. Cæsarius, he banished demons and wrought miracles that echoed through the ages. His staff, a conduit of heavenly power, trembled at his command, casting out darkness with each ethereal stroke.

St. Giles, stalwart amid the shadows of a secluded cave, was cradled by a mystical hind, nourished by her miraculous milk. Bound by a bond unseen, he shielded his gentle companion from the fangs of ravenous hounds, drawing lines of sanctity that even beasts of fury dared not cross, bearing witness to his holy might.

The tale of St. Euphemia, encompassed by angels in celestial armor, transcends mortal comprehension. Ensnared by foes intent on her demise, she emerged unscathed from the inferno's grasp, untouched by flames that consumed her assailants. Even nature itself bowed in deference, as beasts in their dens turned away, and iron lost its edge in her presence, marking her as a vessel of divine protection until her martyrdom, met with unyielding grace.

St. Francis, borne aloft in a chariot ablaze, beheld a city torn asunder by strife, where malicious spirits reveled in chaos. With resounding authority, he castigated the demons, banishing discord in a crescendo of divine command that restored peace to the beleaguered streets.

St. Bridget, blessed with visions of seraphic angels, walked amidst both ethereal splendor and harrowing trials. Confronted by Satan himself, a grotesque fiend with myriad limbs, she sought refuge in the sanctum of a holy relic, where she found sanctuary from the horrors that beset her. In moments of despair, the spirit of St. Denis emerged, pledging eternal protection, as she wielded miraculous powers: restoring sight to the blind, speech to the mute, and life to the lifeless, sanctified by Pope Boniface IX in solemn recognition of her miraculous deeds.

St. Gregory of Tours recounted the radiant deeds of St. Denis, where miracles transcended the boundaries of life and death. St. Teresa, graced by celestial visions and attended by angels of resplendent form, brandished a flaming sword against adversity, a sentinel from the order of the Seraphim, guarding her in perilous hours. With unyielding faith in the sanctity of holy water, she purged the infernal legions as a mighty river sweeps away debris.

Thus, amidst the tapestry of saints, their epics resound with awe and dread, a testament to divine might and providence that echoes through the corridors of time, beckoning mortals to witness the eternal struggle between light and shadow, sanctity and damnation.

In the days of legend and darkness, St. Hilarian stood as a formidable adversary to the forces of Satan and his dark cabal of sorcerers. A young man, driven by an unquenchable desire for a maiden of ethereal beauty and virtue, sought the aid of sorcerers who served the ancient temple of Esculapius. Through their malevolent arts, the maiden's heart was ensnared, but not with love true and pure—rather, a frenzied obsession that bordered on madness. Her anguished parents, desperate and fearful, brought her plight to St. Hilarian's feet.

With divine authority and courage that echoed through the ages, St. Hilarian banished the malevolent spirit that had ensnared the maiden, both body and soul. Yet, his actions were not always seen as salvation. Once, when the parched lands beseeched him for rain, he granted their wish, but the skies opened to unleash not water, but a torrent teeming with serpents and venomous creatures. These abominations ravaged the crops and afflicted the people with their deadly sting. Undeterred, akin to the valiant St. Patrick of old, St. Hilarian cleansed the land of these serpentine horrors and healed those who had suffered their wrath.

Yet, his legendary feats did not end there. In a feat

of unparalleled bravery and divine power, St. Hilarian confronted and vanquished a monstrous dragon of colossal proportions. This beast, with jaws that devoured oxen whole and laid waste to the fertile lands, met its end in a blaze of holy fire conjured by the saint's righteous hand. The land rejoiced in awe and terror at the heroism of St. Hilarian, whose name resounded across the ages as a beacon of light in the encroaching darkness.

Similarly, St. Martin, blessed with the miraculous gift to restore life to the dead, wielded dominion over both the celestial and terrestrial realms. His authority extended over angels and demons alike, over the heavens and the tempestuous elements, over diseases that plagued mortal flesh, and over all creatures that roam the earth.

The purity and sanctity of St. Catherine transcended mortal reckoning. Upon her death, celestial beings bore her incorruptible body to the sacred heights of Mount Sinai, concealing her resting place from those who sought to desecrate her memory. A fragrance of unearthly sweetness emanated from her tomb, a testament to her holiness that lingered in the air, sanctifying the land for generations to come.

Indeed, each saint possessed unique gifts and graces, bestowed upon them by divine providence. St. Francis Xaverius, for instance, commanded the very elements themselves, wielding them against the forces of darkness that perpetually assailed him. His nights were a ceaseless vigil against the temptations of the devil, the unyielding peal of his bell warding off evil spirits. In penance and asceticism, he subdued the desires of the flesh, clad in a hair shirt, subsisting on meager sustenance, and finding respite only upon the harsh embrace of unforgiving earth.

Thus, in an epoch where miracles and marvels were wrought by the hands of these holy champions, their lives and deeds reverberate through time, inspiring awe and fear in equal measure, their legacies woven into the very fabric of myth and faith.

In ages past, amidst the shadows of history, there

arose saints whose faith burned like a thousand suns, their deeds echoing through eternity with epic and eerie resonance.

St. Nicholas, from his very infancy, shunned the ordinary for the extraordinary. Even at his mother's breast, he defied hunger, taking nourishment only on solemn Wednesdays and Fridays. But his greatness did not end there. He commanded the elements themselves, taming the raging winds and commanding the tumultuous seas, driving the malevolent spirits before him, howling in despair through the tempest.

St. Ambrose, blessed with eternal memory, held dominion over sorcerers and necromancers alike. His very presence struck fear into the hearts of demons, who on the day of his passing fled, shrieking in torment at his righteous wrath.

St. Lucy, in a display of unearthly power, raised her own mother from the cold grip of death and waged victorious battle against the forces of darkness.

St. Anastasia, wielding celestial authority, subdued Satan himself and for two months sustained her earthly form with bread from heaven.

And what of St. Thomas, Archbishop of Canterbury, who twice endured martyrdom—for his faith in life and again in death? He scourged his flesh until rivers of blood marked his devotion, keeping vigil through long and lonely nights, clad in the penitent's hair shirt. In a prophetic vision, he foresaw his martyrdom, a prophecy that crimsoned the annals of the Church.

Yet, even in death, his sanctity was not spared the cruelty of kings. Henry II, implicated in his demise, groveled in penance, seeking absolution for his grave sin. Centuries later, the wrathful Henry VIII, in a vengeful act of defiance, condemned the saint as a traitor. He ordered St. Thomas' name erased from every sacred scroll and calendar, his relics consigned to flames, their ashes scattered upon the winds.

Thus, the tales of these saints resonate through

time, their epic deeds and eerie trials bearing witness to the eternal struggle between light and shadow, faith and doubt, in the grand tapestry of human destiny.

In the annals of Demonology, there exists a tale so ancient and chilling that it defies the boundaries of mortal comprehension. This saga, born from the depths of human fear, resonates with the echoes of a bygone era—a time when superstition held sway over the souls of men and the very air thrummed with eerie premonitions.

Not more than a century and a half ago, amidst the remote villages of Sclavonia, these events unfolded like a macabre symphony conducted by fate itself. What began as whispers among peasants soon became a thunderous truth, haunting the valleys and hills with its dread presence. Even the learned minds of divines and physicians, once stalwart in their skepticism, found themselves ensnared in its web of terror.

Behold, as I recount the saga, woven in verse, of those haunted days. I traversed lands far and wide, from the chalky cliffs of ancient England to the sacred realms of Greece and beyond, until my journey led me to the somber heart of Hungary. There, amidst the proud walls and towering mosques of Pest, I encountered sights that would etch themselves into the very fabric of my being.

Picture a city of grandeur, yet cloaked in a veil of foreboding. Its streets, once bustling with life, now lay abandoned, overgrown with spectral grass that whispered secrets of the damned. Even on a Sabbath day, no church bells rang to summon the faithful, for the air itself seemed to reject the presence of mortals.

In this desolate place, I chanced upon an old man, his visage etched with sorrow deeper than the Danube's waters. His voice, hollow as the grave, pierced through my soul as he warned me in the name of Mary to flee this accursed land. Yet, curiosity bound me to him, and I implored him to reveal the secrets that lay buried beneath Pest's melancholy facade.

"It is morn," he intoned, "and the sun shines

bright, yet within Pest's walls, a deeper darkness stirs. Were it a wild winter's night with storms raging, even then, stranger, you would find no solace here."

Undeterred, I pressed him further, and thus began his tale—a tale of woe that transcended mere mortal suffering. He spoke of a once-thriving city now gripped by a mysterious affliction, where the vibrant cheeks of youth turned pallid and robust spirits succumbed to unrelenting chills.

Weeks turned into a season of despair as the town's folk withered away, their bodies betraying them as if drained of life itself. Physicians theorized, theologians prayed, yet none could fathom the true nature of the malady that plagued them. It was whispered that the lakes bred agues, while others proclaimed the heat itself a harbinger of doom.

But amidst this epidemic of fear, a tailor named Vulvius met an end that defied all reason. In death, he rose from his grave, a revenant clad in burial shroud, haunting the very stairways of his former abode. His spectral visits, witnessed by trembling eyes, bespoke a horror that no mortal tongue could adequately describe.

Driven by dread, the old man and I embarked on a quest for answers, delving into the darkness that gripped Pest like a vise. We unearthed the tailor's coffin, expecting decay but finding instead a macabre tableau—a corpse seemingly nourished on fresh blood, a daughter's blood.

Word spread like wildfire through the town, igniting a panic that consumed even the bravest souls. The undead, it was declared, had taken root in their midst, feasting on the lifeblood of the innocent. Churchyards became battlegrounds, where the living fought to secure their dead from unholy resurrection.

Priests invoked ancient rites, burning incense to cleanse the sanctuaries and casting the profane into the depths of the Danube. Yet, iron bolts could not bar the restless dead, for when a man learns to defy death itself, no earthly barrier can restrain his hunger.

Silent, the old man's tale concluded, leaving me with a burden of grief and horror that clung to my very soul. Nine leagues I rode that night, fleeing the cursed walls of Pest, yet in my heart, the specter of that tale would forever haunt my dreams.

Made in the USA
Middletown, DE
09 October 2024

62308006R00066